HELLO, BEE!

Every day, billions of bees visit flowers, buzzing loudly as they busily collect nectar and pollen. These remarkable insects do an important job, and we depend on them for our survival. Discover the incredible story of how bees live and what we can do to help them thrive in our changing world.

There are about 21,000 species of bees in the world and most of them are solitary bees, which means they live alone. The largest bee in the world, Wallace's giant bee, has an impressive wingspan of 63 millimetres. The smallest bee, *Quasihesma clypearis*, however, is just 1.8 millimetres long!

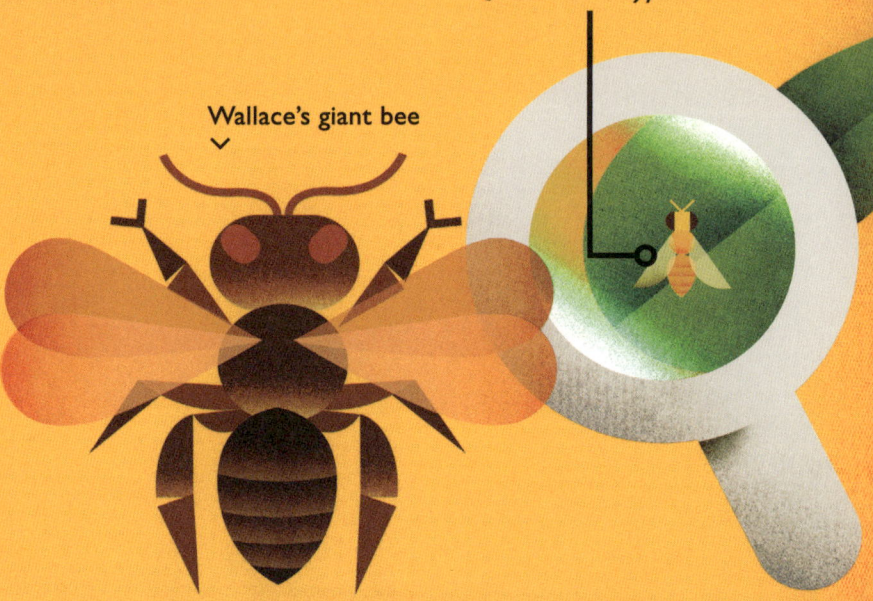

Quasihesma clypearis

Wallace's giant bee

BEE FAMILY

There are four main types of bees: solitary bees, bumblebees, stingless bees and honeybees. They are further divided into smaller groups by their appearance and how closely related they are to each other, for example: mining bees, carpenter bees and sweat bees.

Honeybees: 8 species
Bumblebees: 250 species
Stingless bees: 500–600 species
Solitary bees: about 19,000 species

ORDER: HYMENOPTERA

SUPERFAMILY: APOIDEA (BEES)

SUPERFAMILY: VESPOIDEA (WASPS)

FAMILY: HALICTIDAE (E.G., SWEAT BEES)

FAMILY: APIDAE (E.G., CARPENTER BEES)

FAMILY: ANDRENIDAE (E.G., MINING BEES)

IS IT A BEE OR A WASP?

Most bees are hairier than wasps, with fuzzy bodies. Wasps usually have smoother, more slender bodies than bees, and a small waist that separates the two main body parts.

Bee

Wasp

WHY DO BEES VISIT FLOWERS?

Bees visit flowers to gather pollen, a yellow dust that flowers make to reproduce, and nectar, a sugary liquid flowers make to attract insects. Bees eat pollen and nectar, and feed them to their young. Honeybees also use nectar to make honey.

BEE BODY BASICS

Bees are insects – a huge and amazing group of animals that have survived for more than 400 million years and now live all over the world. Insects are successful because their bodies can be adapted to suit almost any habitat and lifestyle.

Compound eye

Antenna

Head

Bees have two sets of wings, unlike flies, which have just one set.

Thorax

Abdomen

Insects have three pairs of legs, at the front, side and back of their bodies. Many bees carry pollen on their hind legs, in 'pollen baskets', or corbiculae.

Stinger

An insect's body is divided into three main parts: the *head*, the *thorax* and the *abdomen*. Wings and legs are attached to the thorax. If a bee has a stinger, it grows from the tip of the abdomen.

A bee has three tiny extra eyes, called ocelli. They help bees find their way in dim light.

Insects use their antennae to touch, smell and taste.

Antenna

Most adult insects have large compound eyes, which are made up of many small lenses. This gives an insect good vision in all directions, but they can't see the colour red.

There are at least 6,000 lenses in each eye and they are all hexagon shaped.

Mouthparts

Insects don't have bony skeletons. Instead they have a tough skin called an exoskeleton. It protects their soft body parts and is often colourful.

The yellow and black bands on a bee warn predators, such as birds, that the bee may sting if it's attacked.

BEE PURPLE

Bees can see colours, such as ultraviolet, that are invisible to humans. They follow the ultraviolet stripes on petals to find nectar at the centre of the flower.

Many bees have a covering of hair-like fuzz. This helps them collect pollen and detect vibrations (see page 11).

HOW BEES LIVE

Bees are busy insects with plenty of work to do. They visit flowers, but they also have nests to build and young to care for.

Bees survive on a special diet of pollen and nectar. They store food in a stretchy stomach-like pouch, called a honey crop.

Nectar can be stored in the honey crop.

POLLEN

Look inside a flower and you will see pollen – a fine, yellow dust. Pollen is good for bees since it contains proteins and fats, which the insects need to grow.

Bees have a long straw-like tongue, called a proboscis, which they use to suck up nectar.

NECTAR

Flowers make nectar to tempt bees and other insects to visit them. The nectar gives insects instant energy, and some bees also use it to make honey. The part of a flower that makes nectar is called a nectary.

Bees prefer mild habitats, which do not get very hot or very cold. Good bee habitats need to have plenty of flowering plants, as well as places where bees can nest, rest and shelter from the weather.

Big, hairy and tough, the Arctic bumblebee keeps warm in its chilly habitat with an extra-thick layer of fuzz that traps heat. It also warms itself up by making its muscles shiver and shake! A queen Arctic bumblebee can sleep for nine months at a time, snug inside a burrow beneath the snow.

While some bees live up to seven years, others live for just two weeks!

Bees collect pollen using special hairs, called scopae, which grow on their legs and abdomen.

A bumblebee

BUSY BEES

Bees love flowers, and flowers love bees! Like the best friendships, they need each other. Since bees first evolved, 120 million years ago, they have been helping flowering plants grow. In return, the flowers have been giving them a lifetime's supply of delicious nectar and pollen.

1 A bee lands on a flower to gather pollen or suck its nectar. As it moves around, pollen gets trapped in the scopae on its body. When the bee flies to another flower, the pollen gets brushed onto the stigma and pollinates the flower.

Petals attract pollinators, but also protect the stigma, ovary and stamen.

Stamen – the male part of a flower, where pollen grows

2 A stamen has pollen on its tip. Pollination happens when pollen reaches the stigma – a female part of the flower.

3 Fertilisation happens when the pollen joins with an egg inside the flower's ovary. Once fertilised, an egg can grow into a seed.

4 A seed must reach a place where it can grow, such as soil. This is called dispersal. Some seeds disperse on the wind, but others are dispersed by animals, such as birds.

Stigma – the female part where pollen lands

Honeybees and bumblebees use scopae, the stiff hairs on their legs, to push pollen grains into special pockets on their legs, or bodies, called pollen baskets. The pollen they can't reach stays on their bodies and pollinates flowers.

Pollen basket (corbicula)

Ovary – the female part where eggs grow

BEE SENSES

Bees see, hear, touch, smell and taste, just like humans. However, they sense the world around them very differently. Because bees can see ultraviolet light, they can spot details that are invisible to us.

A bee can use its antennae to 'sniff' the air and find sweet-smelling flowers.

Antennae

Like other insects, bees have special feelers on their head, called antennae. They are supersensitive to smells in the air, in liquid or on flowers. Bees constantly touch things, including each other, with their antennae.

Bees do not have ears, but they can hear. They have special places on their antennae that pick up sounds. They probably use their hearing to listen for signs of danger, and to listen to other bees buzzing.

A bee's body is covered in hairs that feel movement and vibrations, which is especially useful inside a dark nest or hive.

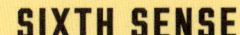

SIXTH SENSE
Honeybees use their special senses to detect thunderstorms far away and return to the safety of their nest before the rain comes.

When a bee pokes its tongue-like proboscis inside a flower, it can taste the sugary nectar inside. Bees can also taste with their antennae and feet!

WHAT'S THE BUZZ!

How do bees find their way?
They probably use a range of senses, including a special super-sense that helps them navigate using the Earth's magnetic field.

Bees use their compound eyes (see page 5) to work out the position of the Sun to decide which direction to travel in, and to spot landmarks, such as trees and rivers.

Their ocelli help them see the horizon, where land meets the sky.

Their sense of smell directs them to flowers and back to their nest.

ON THE WING

In the past, scientists couldn't understand how bumblebees could fly. Their muscles and wings did not seem big and strong enough to lift them up into the air, especially when a big bumblebee was carrying pollen.

Now we know that all bees fly by twisting their flapping wings to create whirling currents of air, called vortices, which give their heavy bodies extra lift.

A wing's joint allows the wing to move forwards, backwards, up and down.

Joint

A WING'S STRUCTURE

A bee's two pairs of wings are attached to the thorax. Each wing is made up of two extremely thin layers, or membranes, with veins running between them.

Thorax

A bee's flight muscles are inside its thorax. The thorax is covered in hairs to keep the muscles warm.

Veins give wings strength and support, allowing them to change shape, fold and flex. They also carry nerves and supplies of oxygen and blood to the wing.

Veins

Forewings

SUPER STRENGTH

Bees may not be very fast or dainty flyers, but they are strong. Some carry loads of pollen and nectar that weigh almost as much as they do!

A row of little hooks, called hamuli, line the edge of each hindwing. They fit into a groove on the forewing, holding the two wings together for extra strength and lift.

Hamuli

Hindwings

Honeybees fly for up to 8 kilometres (5 miles) in a single trip. That means, adding all their journeys together, a colony of 50,000 honeybees could fly the same distance as the journey from Earth to the Moon every day!

BODY TALK

Some bees live as members of big families, called colonies. They share daily tasks, such as building a nest or hive and caring for the eggs and young bees. Working together is difficult unless you communicate, so these social bees have some clever ways of 'talking' to each other.

Bees make smell-chemicals called pheromones, which other bees sense with their antennae. Pheromones help bees recognise one another, but bees can also make pheromones to send a message, such as 'come here' or 'fly away, there's danger about!'

Bees that live together in colonies are called social bees. While many species of bees nest together, social bees are special because their colonies are more organised. They share the work that needs to be done, with some bees laying eggs while others collect food. Honeybees, bumblebees, and some carpenter bees and sweat bees, can live this way.

Bumblebees also use their wings to communicate with each other.

Did you know that honeybees dance? They use smells, sounds and two special dances to tell each other where to find food:

WAGGLE DANCE

When the food is more than 50 metres away, a honeybee does a waggle dance. She moves in a figure-of-eight pattern and waggles her abdomen to tell her hive-mates where they will find the food.

ROUND DANCE

A honeybee walks round and round in circles, changing direction to tell her hive-mates that there is a supply of food to be found less than 50 metres away. At the end of the dance, she gives the other bees a tasty sample of the nectar and pollen she has found, and they go off to gather more.

THE FRIENDLY BEE

Honeybees are found all over the world. They are friends to people and animals, helping farmers pollinate their crops and making honey that people and animals eat. Honeybees have big families.

There can be more than 50,000 honeybees in a colony, especially in the summer. They live in either a human-made hive or a natural nest, where they store food and raise young bees (called larvae).

Many people think honeybees are yellow and black, but a healthy colony has bees with a mix of colours. The darker bands on their abdomen can be black, grey, or brown and the lighter bands yellow or orange.

The **queen bee** is the mother of all the other bees in her hive. She is the largest bee in the colony and the only one that lays eggs.

Most honeybees are worker bees. These females do almost all of the work in the nest, including feeding the queen and the drones, but their jobs change as they get older.

Keeping cool
Worker bees keep beating their wings to move air around the nest, keeping their home cool and fresh.

Nurses
Young worker bees take care of eggs and larvae. They also clean the hive and remove any dead bees.

Guards and chefs
At two to three weeks old, workers guard the hive to stop intruders from entering. They also make honey, store pollen and keep the nest at a perfect temperature.

Foragers
Only older worker bees (about three weeks old) leave the hive in search of food and water.

Drones are male bees and there are usually just a few hundred of them in a nest or hive. They are bigger than workers, with very large eyes. Drones have one job to do: they mate with a new queen, and they die as soon as they have completed this task.

A HONEYBEE'S LIFE CYCLE

Many adult insects – including bees – look very different when they are young. The story of how an animal grows and changes is called a life cycle. There are four stages in a bee's life cycle, starting with an egg.

EGG

The queen lays eggs. The place where a bee lays her eggs is called a brood chamber. Most eggs have been fertilised by males and will grow into female bees. Some eggs, however, are not fertilised and they grow into drones, which are male.

LARVA

The eggs hatch and a small, soft grub called a larva emerges from each one. Adult worker bees make a special food in their body for the larvae, called brood food, and bring them pollen and honey to eat.

The workers feed all larvae with special food, called royal jelly, for a short while. The healthiest larva is given extra portions for longer and she will grow bigger, eventually becoming a queen bee.

QUEEN BEE

A honeybee queen can lay up to 2,000 eggs a day. Most lay eggs for one to two years, but some survive for up to seven years.

PUPA

The larva makes silk and spins itself a special silken case, called a cocoon. The bee's body begins to develop legs, wings and other body parts. It is called a pupa at this stage.

ADULT

Around twelve days later, the young bee chews away the lid of its cell and climbs out, ready to begin its adult life.

Each pupa is safe inside a cell made of wax. Worker bees make a lid for each cell.

HIVES AND HONEY

A honeybee's natural home is a nest, which the bees usually build in a tree hollow where it will be warm and dry in the winter. Honeybees also live in beehives, which are made by people so they can harvest the honey and wax that bees make.

Inside the nest or hive there are honeycombs, which are made of beeswax that has been moulded into hexagon-shaped cells. The honeybees store honey and pollen in the cells, and the queen lays eggs in other cells, called brood cells.

Some worker bees make beeswax using pollen and special wax flakes that are made in their abdomen. Other worker bees collect the beeswax to build more cells.

Honey is made from nectar. A worker bee brings nectar back to the nest in her honey crop and another bee takes it from her and spreads it over the honeycomb. Bees beat their wings over the honeycomb to dry the nectar until it turns into thick, syrupy honey. The cells are then sealed with wax lids.

WHAT'S THE BUZZ?

Why do bees make honey?
Honeybees make honey so they have a store of food for the winter.

Who eats honey?
Bees and humans love honey, but other animals do too! Bears, badgers, skunks and raccoons all raid honeybee nests for their sweet treats, as well as several types of birds and bugs.

SWARM!

A huge group of honeybees leaves the hive and takes to the air, busily buzzing as they follow their queen. This is a bee swarm, and it is one of nature's most awesome sights. Working as a team, the bees are about to start a new colony. Only honeybees create swarms.

1 When a honeybee colony gets too big, it needs to split into two. The worker bees begin to raise a new queen, choosing one larva to feed with royal jelly. When it hatches, the new queen will be ready to take over the hive, while the old queen prepares to move out.

2 Up to 500 scout bees leave the hive to start searching for the perfect new home. Tens of thousands of bees and the old queen follow the scouts out of the hive and settle nearby, often clustered together high up on the branch of a tree. They rest and wait for the scouts to give them instructions on where to fly next.

3 Once a scout has found a site, it returns to the cluster of bees and does a special dance to tell other bees to visit the site. If they like it, these bees also start to dance. When enough bees have joined in the dance, all the bees take to the air, swarming in a huge dark cloud as they make their way to their new home.

A NEW FAMILY

The new queen stays in the old hive, with about half of the colony's original bees. She may live for up to seven years, laying thousands of eggs to build the colony up to a good size again.

BEE CAREFUL!

Many bees have a nasty weapon — a venomous stinger at the tip of the abdomen. Bees are usually calm, peaceful insects, but if they are attacked, they can be quick to sting.

A bee's stinger is at the tip of its abdomen. Only female bees have stingers, and some bees, called stingless bees, don't sting at all!

^
Stingless bee

WARNING!
Bee stings are painful, but some people are allergic to bee venom when stung. Always keep a safe distance from a bee, and never try to touch a bee or go close to its nest.

A honeybee's stinger is barbed, so it gets stuck in skin and stays there while venom is pumped into the wound. The bee cannot pull its stinger out, so it gets torn from the bee's body and the bee dies.

This means that honeybees can only sting once.

The Asian giant hornet grows up to 5 centimetres long and can kill a thousand honeybees in a single attack on a hive, usually by biting off the bees' heads with its powerful mandibles.

1 2 3 4 5 6 7 8

Hornets attack honeybees to raid the honey and larvae in their nest. Honeybees defend their home by swarming around the invader and beating their wings fast to create a deadly heat ball. This makes enough heat to kill the hornet!

WHAT'S THE BUZZ?

Why do bees buzz?
Buzzing warns people and other animals to keep a safe distance from a bee, even if they can't see it. The buzzing sound is made by their wings as they beat 230 times a second.

DIGGER BEES

There are about 800 species of digger bees, so-called because they dig holes for their nests in the soil, old wood or even walls. Digger bees are often shiny or metallic and the males have unusually large antennae.

Digger bees are important pollinators, and they live all over the world. Although they are solitary bees, females often gather in groups to nest.

This beautiful, fluffy digger bee is timid and rarely stings so it deserves its cuddly name of teddy bear bee! It lives in Australasia and builds its nest in riverbanks or soil, usually choosing places that are well hidden from view.

Golden-brown fuzzy body

Females have six dark bands on their abdomens, but males have seven.

CARPENTER BEES

Carpenter bees have large, strong mandibles (jaws) which they use to munch wood, making holes to lay their eggs in. Females work hard to defend their nests by buzzing loudly and flying at any attackers, but they are no match for woodpeckers that spot these telltale holes. The birds peck away at the holes with their strong beaks until they can reach the eggs and larvae deep inside.

Shiny abdomen, mostly hairless

WHAT'S THE BUZZ?

How many types of carpenter bee are there?
There are at least 400 species of carpenter bees.

Where do they live?
Worldwide, except Antarctica.

ORCHID BEES

With rainbow colours, these insects are the brilliant jewels of the bee family. Orchid bees are the only living things, apart from humans, that are known to collect 'smells' to make perfume. There are about 250 species of orchid bees.

Orchid flowers grow in tropical rainforests. Male orchid bees collect their fragrances in special chambers on their hind legs and add other ingredients, such as fruit, to create the best-smelling perfume. Once the bee is happy with his smell, he flies around a female bee in the hope that she will choose to mate with him.

< Green orchid bee

Orchids make a range of smells to tempt bees to visit them. As a bee burrows into the flower to reach the scents, the flower drops pollen on his back. He flies to the next flower and pollinates it.

MASTER PERFUMERS

Male orchid bees fly far to create the best perfume. A single trip may cover 48 kilometres (30 miles)!

CUCKOO BEES

Being a parent is tough, especially for female bees that do all the hard work of building nests, laying eggs and finding food. Like the cuckoo bird who lays its eggs in other birds' nests, cuckoo bees use the same trick to avoid having to take care of their own young.

The domino cuckoo bee lives in Australia. It lays its eggs in the nest of the teddy bear bee (see page 27).

Up to one third of all bee species are cuckoo bees. Their larvae normally hatch before the other bees' larvae and eat all their food.

< Domino cuckoo bee

MINING BEES

Digging a nest in the ground is a good way of hiding eggs and larvae from predators. Mining bees prefer dry habitats with plenty of open ground where they can dig their nest tunnels. The largest mining bees can dig tunnels up to 3 metres underground!

Mining bees have slender bodies and look more wasp-like than other bees. Some mining bees stay in their underground nests for up to three years.

WHAT'S THE BUZZ?

What are they?
Mining bees belong to a large group of solitary bees called Andrenidae.

Where do they live?
Most places, except Australia.

How big are they?
Some species grow as big as bumblebees, but this group also includes some of the world's smallest bees.

This tiny bee is called *Perdita minima* and it measures just 2 millimetres long, making it one of the world's smallest bees. It lives in sandy deserts in North America. Perdita bees are gentle insects, and most types cannot sting.

PLASTERER BEES

Plasterer bees have a clever trick to keep their eggs clean, healthy and dry. Before laying their eggs, female plasterer bees use their short, forked tongues to line their nests with a special liquid that is made in their abdomens. As the liquid dries it turns hard, like plaster on a wall. It is waterproof and stops fungi from growing, which could harm the eggs and larvae.

Like other plasterer bees, the ivy bee collects pollen on its hairy hind legs rather than in a pollen basket.

Ivy bee >

Masked bees, so called because of the yellow markings on their black faces, are close cousins of the plasterer bees. They look like tiny, smooth wasps and instead of collecting pollen on their bodies, they swallow it and carry it back to the nest in their stomachs.

LEAFCUTTER, WOOL-CARDER AND MASON BEES

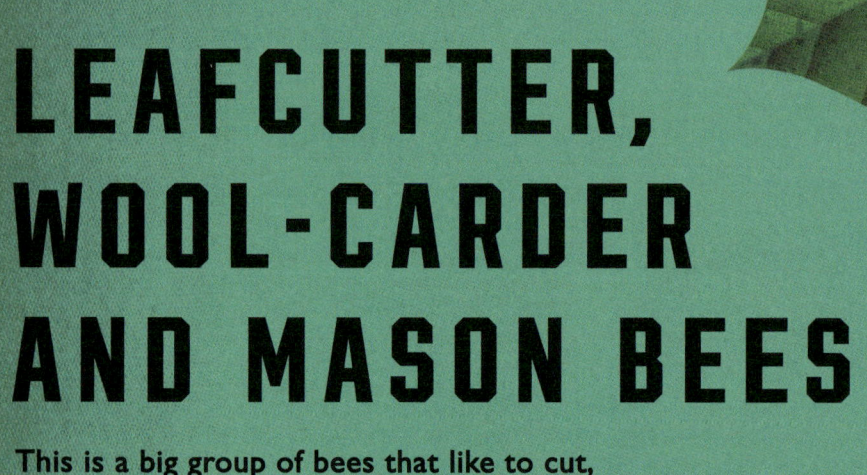

This is a big group of bees that like to cut, collect and craft materials to make their nests. They usually have large jaws and collect pollen on their undersides, instead of their legs.

A female alfalfa leafcutter bee uses her scissor-like jaws to cut leaves into small pieces and chews their edges to make them sticky. She sticks the leaves together to build chambers in her nest, where the bee lays her eggs.

The female wool-carder bee scrapes tiny, soft hairs from the leaves of plants and gathers them into a bundle. She carries them back to her nest and uses them to line her egg chambers.

Blobs of mud and clay make good building materials for a nest, so mason bees often use them to seal up each egg cell, protecting the growing larvae and keeping them warm.

MASTER BUILDERS

Bees in this big family are master builders. Some species use the sticky resin and sap from plants to build their nests, while others use mud or small pebbles.

A female red mason bee uses peg-like horns on her face to mould mud along the walls of her nest's tunnel, and another spiral-shaped blob to seal its entrance shut, keeping pests out.

Some mason bees, such as poppy bees, line their brood chambers with mud and flower petals, which are stuck together with nectar. It takes a poppy bee four weeks to build her nest and lay her eggs. She dies of exhaustion soon afterwards.

34

BUMBLEBEES

Fuzzy, buzzy bumblebees fly in a haphazard, almost 'bumbling' way as they travel between flowers. There are about 250 different species of bumblebees, and they are common in places that have cold winter weather. Bumblebees' large, hairy bodies help to keep them warm.

Like their honeybee cousins, bumblebees are social bees. In spring, a queen bumblebee wakes from her winter sleep to make a nest where she lays eggs, which hatch into worker bees. They find food and look after the queen, her eggs and the larvae.

In autumn, the queen and all the worker bees die, but the colony now includes new queens and male drones. They leave the nest and mate. The drones die after mating, but the young queens will spend the winter resting somewhere warm and dry.

The garden bumblebee lives in Europe and Asia. Workers measure up to 16 millimetres long.

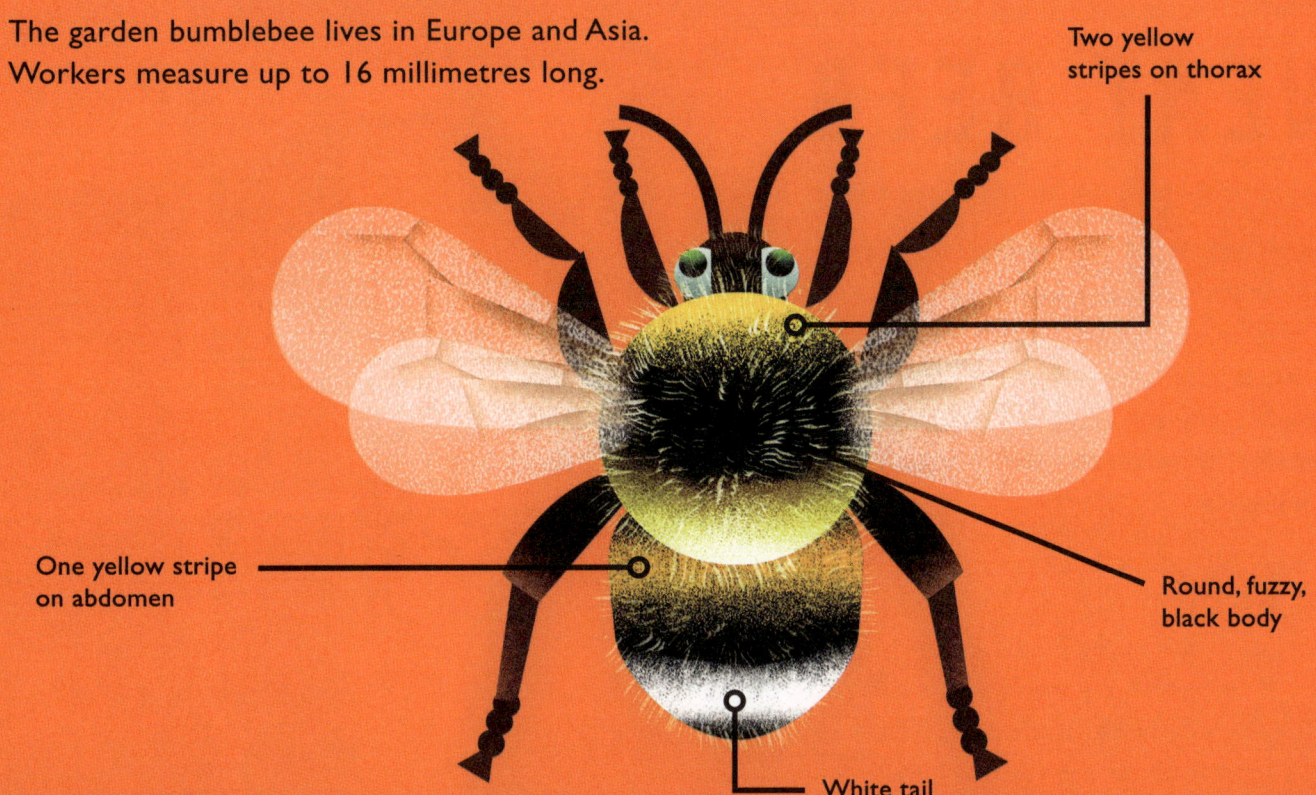

Two yellow stripes on thorax

One yellow stripe on abdomen

Round, fuzzy, black body

White tail

BUZZING BEES

Bumblebees pollinate flowers when they collect nectar and pollen. They have a special skill called 'buzz pollination'. Bumblebees grab hold of certain flowers in their jaws or claws and vibrate their wing muscles to produce a loud 'buzz'. This forces the flowers to release their pollen, making it easier to gather.

WHAT'S THE BUZZ?

Bumblebee identifcation:
You can identify many species of bumblebees by their colours. This type of bee grows up to 17 millimetres long, but queens are slightly bigger.

Tree bumblebees have a ginger, fluffy thorax and white tail. They live in Europe and often nest in trees and bird boxes.

Common eastern bumblebees live in North America. They have creamy gold hair on the thorax.

Buff-tailed bumblebees live in Europe, Asia and North Africa. They have a golden yellow band near the head and another on the abdomen. The tip of the tail is white.

SWEAT BEES

Sweat bees are not fussy feeders! They are happy to visit almost any type of flower and take its nectar and pollen, which they store in their nests for their larvae to eat. While some sweat bees are small and dark, others have metallic, shiny bodies that gleam like precious jewels.

BABY BEES

In the spring or summer, female sweat bees dig holes in soil and lay a single egg inside each cell. When the bee larvae hatch from their eggs they feed on the food left by their mother, and grow bigger.

The larvae usually pupate and turn into adults during the same year, but if the weather turns cold they wait until the following spring to pupate. Some adults spend the winter in the nest, waiting for warmer weather to come in springtime.

UNUSUAL NAME
Sweat bees in hot climates like the salty taste of human sweat, and sometimes lick skin! That's how they got their strange name.

When the female makes her nest, she puts pollen and nectar in each cell for her larvae. Adult sweat bees only eat nectar.

BRIGHT BEES

Metallic sweat bees are usually blue or green. They often live alone, but some types share a nest underground where they each lay an egg on a ball of pollen. These colourful bees live in the Americas.

Females are often blue or green all over, but males may have stripes. Females collect pollen on hairs on their hind legs.

BEWARE

Blood bees are a type of black sweat bee with a red abdomen. They are aggressive bees who invade other bees' nests. They kill the eggs or larvae before laying their own eggs inside the cells and sealing them up again.

BEE-UTIFUL WILD FLOWERS

Sweat bees love the nectar from fruit trees and wildflowers. They have short tongues, so they avoid trumpet-shaped flowers that have nectar tucked deep inside. Sweat bees prefer to nest alone, or in small groups, under bare soil in a sunny place.

WHAT'S THE BUZZ?

What are sweat bees?
A group of about 4,200 types of bees, which are also known as halictids.

Where do they live?
Worldwide, especially in warm and cool places.

What do they eat?
Nectar from different flowers and trees.

Where do they nest?
Usually underground.

KEEPING BEES

A beekeeper is a person who has at least one colony of honeybees living in a beehive. Since ancient times, people have kept bees for their honey, beeswax and honeycomb, and to pollinate their crops.

FARMERS AND BEES

Farmers need bees to visit their crops to pollinate their flowers, so the flowers can then grow fruit, vegetables, nuts, seeds and even more plants! Keeping beehives on a farm means farmers can grow more food for us to eat – a third of the food we eat comes from plants pollinated by bees!

GARDENERS AND BEES

Many gardeners grow small crops of fruit and vegetables to eat, as well as flowers to enjoy. Keeping a beehive can be a fun hobby for gardeners, and helps them to grow more plants.

KEEPING BEES

Beekeepers need to check their beehives regularly, making sure the beehive is in good shape, the bees are healthy and there are no signs of infection or disease. When they collect honey, beekeepers make sure that the bees still have enough food for the colony.

KEEPING SAFE

Bees can sting, especially when someone opens up their hive to take honey!

Beekeepers need special equipment to keep safe:

 **A beekeeping suit gives protection from hot weather and bee stings**

 **Gloves allow beekeepers to handle equipment in the hive**

 **Helmets with a veil protect the face**

 **Hive tools are used to open the hive and lift out the frames**

 **A bee brush helps to gently remove bees from the honeycomb**

 **A smoker is used to calm the bees**

BEES AND SMOKE

Bees make pheromones when they need to tell other bees to attack. Puffs of smoke, from a smoker, stop bees from smelling the pheromones, so they stay calm while the beekeeper checks the hive.

BEES IN PERIL

Bees are struggling to survive in many places. Beekeepers have seen their honeybee colonies suddenly shrink, with worker bees disappearing from the nests – and the numbers of wild bees are falling too. Climate change, disease and the loss of habitats are just some of the many reasons that bees are in peril.

HABITATS UNDER THREAT

When wild areas are turned into farms and roads, or built on, the millions of animals and plants that live there lose their homes. This is called habitat loss, and it has badly affected bees as well as many other pollinators.

PESTICIDES

Some farmers and gardeners use pesticides to control the bugs that attack their crops. The problem is, these chemicals kill lots of insects that do no harm at all, including bees.

POLLUTION

Air pollution is dirty air caused by burning fossil fuels and other chemicals. Air pollution makes it more difficult for bees to communicate with each other. It also damages the plants that bees feed on.

CLIMATE CHANGE

Humans have been changing the world's climate by burning fossil fuels. A warmer world does not suit all bees, especially bumblebees, which can quickly overheat and die in unusually hot summers.

TINY TERROR

Bees are under attack from Varroa mites, a type of pest that feeds on other animals. These parasites live inside bees' nests, sucking the blood out of larvae and spreading diseases. They also live on adult bees, using their mouthparts to feed on their hosts.

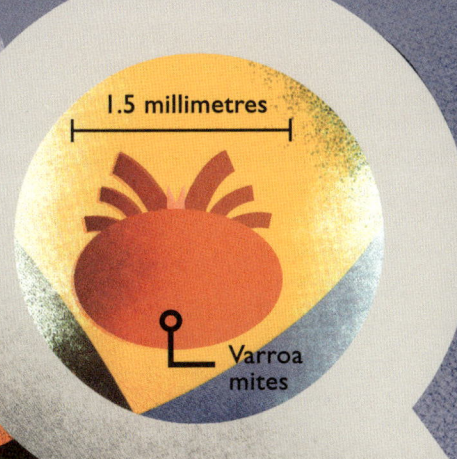

1.5 millimetres

Varroa mites

Bees that have been attacked by *Varroa* mites can have deformed wings. >

BEE AMAZING!

Everyone can help to make the world a better, safer place for bees to live. Even simple things, such as making a home for bees and planting wildflowers can make a difference.

BEE HOTELS

Make or buy a 'bee hotel'. These nest boxes have plenty of holes where solitary bees can nest. They should be placed 1–2 metres off the ground, ideally sheltered from the worst winter weather.

WOOD IS GOOD

Create log piles in cool, dark places. Leave them, undisturbed, and over time they will become a snug winter home for many bugs, including hibernating bees.

MUD PIES

Mason bees are found across the Northern Hemisphere. They need wet mud. In hot weather, put out a plate of wet mud and keep it moist so the bees can collect their building materials.

GROW BEE-FRIENDLY PLANTS

Bees love flowers, especially plants that have single and open flowers, which are easy for bees to pollinate. Growing native wildflowers is best – these are plants that grow naturally in your local habitat. They are the bees' favourites.

LEARN MORE ABOUT BEES

Watch bees at work, but always stay a safe distance away. Take photographs, and use them to identify the bees and learn their names. Make notes of what you see: what is the weather like; what plants are bees visiting; how long do they spend at each flower? What other animals live in the habitat you are observing?

BEE GREEN

We can all do more to cut down our use of fossil fuels. This will help to reduce the damage done by climate change and pollution. Walk or take public transport whenever you can, recycle and reuse the materials that you use, such as plastic and paper, and bee amazing by being kind to nature – especially to our precious bees.

GLOSSARY

Abdomen
The part of an insect's body where digestion takes place

Antenna
One of two feelers on an insect's head. Antennae are used to touch, taste and smell

Beeswax
A wax made by a bee's body and used to make honeycombs

Brood chamber
The place where bees lay their eggs

Cell
Part of the honeycomb where an egg is laid

Cocoon
A case made by an insect larva, where it becomes a pupa and then an adult

Colony
A group of insects that share their home and their work

Crop
Plants that are grown on a farm (e.g., crops of corn or wheat)

Drone
A male bee

Evolve
To change over time

Fertilise
When a male fertilises a female egg it grows into a new living thing

Forage
To search for food

Fossil fuels
Fuels that make pollution, such as coal, oil and gas. They were formed underground from plant and animal remains millions of years ago

Fungi
A type of living thing that makes spores instead of seeds, and feeds on other living or dead things. Mushrooms are a type of fungi

Habitat
Where an animal or plant lives

Hive
A structure built for bees to live in

Hornet
A large type of wasp

Larva
A young insect

Mite
A tiny member of the arachnid (spider) group of animals

Nectar
Sugary liquid made by flowers

Nest
A place that an animal builds for its eggs or young

Ocelli
Small insect eyes

Oxygen
The gas that animals and humans breathe to stay alive

Parasite
An animal or pest that lives on another animal and does it harm

Pheromone
A special chemical that animals make to communicate with each other

Pollen
A fine yellow dust made by the male parts of a flower